D1712539

CASSINI

UNLOCKING THE SECRETS OF SATURN

By John Hamilton

XTREME SPACECRAFT

A&D Xtreme
An imprint of Abdo Publishing | abdopublishing.com

abdopublishing.com

Published by Abdo Publishing, a division of ABDO, PO Box 398166, Minneapolis, Minnesota 55439. Copyright ©2018 by Abdo Consulting Group, Inc. International copyrights reserved in all countries. No part of this book may be reproduced in any form without written permission from the publisher. A&D Xtreme™ is a trademark and logo of Abdo Publishing.

Printed in the United States of America, North Mankato, MN.
042017
052017

THIS BOOK CONTAINS RECYCLED MATERIALS

Editor: Sue Hamilton
Graphic Design: Sue Hamilton
Cover Design: Candice Keimig
Cover Photo: iStock
Interior Photos & Illustrations: NASA

Websites
To learn more about Xtreme Spacecraft, visit abdobooklinks.com. These links are routinely monitored and updated to provide the most current information available.

Publisher's Cataloging-in-Publication Data

Names: Hamilton, John, author.
Title: Cassini: unlocking the secrets of Saturn / by John Hamilton.
Other titles: Unlocking the secrets of Saturn
Description: Minneapolis, MN : Abdo Publishing, 2018. | Series: Xtreme
    spacecraft | Includes index.
Identifiers: LCCN 2016962228 | ISBN 9781532110115 (lib. bdg.) |
    ISBN 9781680787962 (ebook)
Subjects: LCSH: Saturn probes--Juvenile literature. | Saturn (Planet)--Exploration-
    -Juvenile literature. | Titan (Satellite)--Exploration--Juvenile literature.
Classification: DDC 629.43--dc23
LC record available at http://lccn.loc.gov/2016962228

CONTENTS

THE RINGED WORLD OF SATURN

Saturn is the farthest planet from the Sun that can be seen on Earth with the naked eye. In 1610, Galileo peered at the gas giant through a telescope. He and other astronomers in the centuries that followed were puzzled by Saturn's rings.

What were the rings made of? How did they get there? In 2004, NASA's unmanned Cassini-Huygens probe began exploring Saturn. During its 13-year-mission, astronomers have learned more about Saturn and its moons than Galileo could ever have imagined.

Saturn is the second-largest planet in the solar system (Jupiter is the largest). If Saturn were hollow, nearly 764 Earths could fit inside. Like Jupiter, Saturn is called a gas giant. It is mostly made of about 96 percent hydrogen and 3 percent helium.

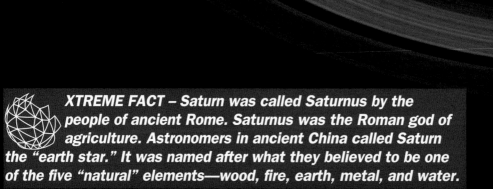

XTREME FACT – Saturn was called Saturnus by the people of ancient Rome. Saturnus was the Roman god of agriculture. Astronomers in ancient China called Saturn the "earth star." It was named after what they believed to be one of the five "natural" elements—wood, fire, earth, metal, and water.

Saturn may have a rocky or liquid metal core. The planet is most famous for its shiny rings. There are seven main rings. They are made mostly of water ice. Saturn has 62 known moons.

PLANNING AND BUILDING

The Cassini-Huygens spacecraft was designed and built by the United States and 16 European countries. Its mission included studying and taking images of Saturn, its rings, and its moons.

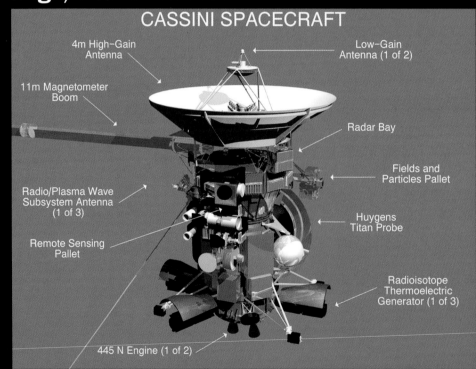

CASSINI SPACECRAFT

4m High–Gain Antenna

Low–Gain Antenna (1 of 2)

11m Magnetometer Boom

Radar Bay

Fields and Particles Pallet

Radio/Plasma Wave Subsystem Antenna (1 of 3)

Huygens Titan Probe

Remote Sensing Pallet

Radioisotope Thermoelectric Generator (1 of 3)

445 N Engine (1 of 2)

XTREME FACT – Cassini was named after Italian astronomer Giovanni Cassini. He studied Saturn, plus its rings and moons, in the late 1600s. The Huygens probe was named after 17th-century Dutch astronomer Christiaan Huygens. He discovered Saturn's moon Titan in 1655.

The bus-sized probe was one of the largest unmanned spacecraft ever built. It had two main parts. The Cassini spacecraft orbited Saturn. The Huygens probe was designed to separate from the main spacecraft. Its mission was to drop by parachute to explore the surface of Titan, Saturn's largest moon.

Cassini is lowered onto its launch vehicle adapter in 1997.

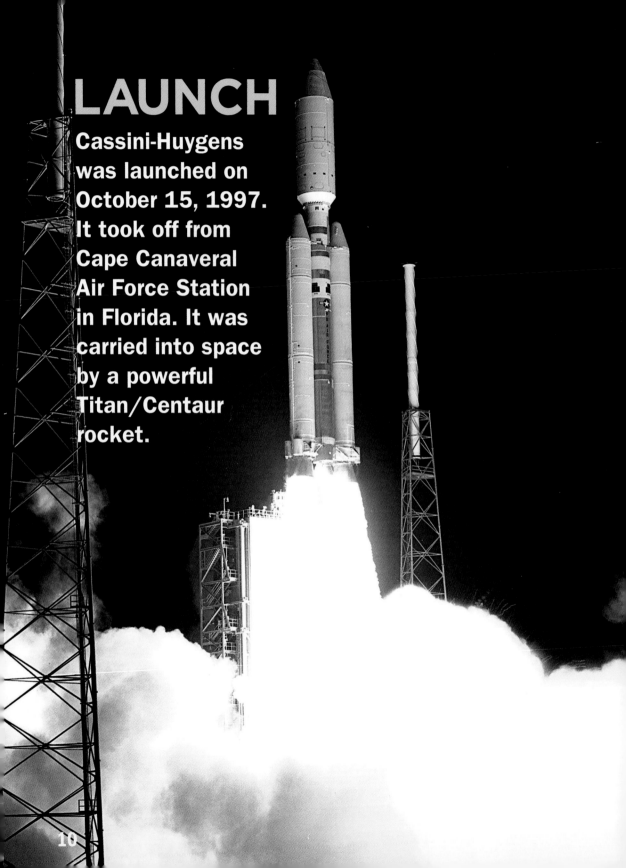

LAUNCH

Cassini-Huygens was launched on October 15, 1997. It took off from Cape Canaveral Air Force Station in Florida. It was carried into space by a powerful Titan/Centaur rocket.

When Earth and Saturn are closest, the two planets are about 746 million miles (1.2 billion km) apart. The Cassini spacecraft's journey, however, was even farther. It first made two flybys of Venus in 1998 and 1999. The planet's gravity gave Cassini-Huygens a speed boost.

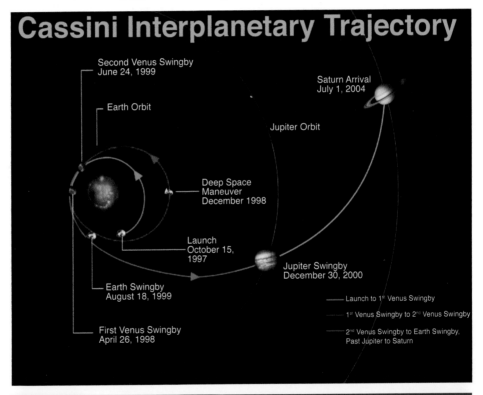

Cassini Interplanetary Trajectory

Second Venus Swingby
June 24, 1999

Saturn Arrival
July 1, 2004

Earth Orbit

Jupiter Orbit

Deep Space
Maneuver
December 1998

Launch
October 15,
1997

Jupiter Swingby
December 30, 2000

Earth Swingby
August 18, 1999

First Venus Swingby
April 26, 1998

Launch to 1st Venus Swingby

1st Venus Swingby to 2nd Venus Swingby

2nd Venus Swingby to Earth Swingby,
Past Jupiter to Saturn

XTREME FACT – The Titan/Centaur used for the Cassini-Huygens spacecraft was a powerful rocket built to carry heavy loads into space. It was developed by the United States Air Force to carry satellites into orbit around Earth.

JUPITER FLYBY

In 1999, Cassini-Huygens made a return visit all the way back to Earth. It used Earth's gravity to boost its speed. While passing close to Earth's Moon, it successfully tested its cameras.

Cassini took photos of Earth's Moon on August 17, 1999.

Jupiter

In early
2000, the
spacecraft safely
passed through the
asteroid belt beyond Mars. In December
2000, Cassini-Huygens made a final planet
flyby, slingshotting past the gas giant Jupiter.

ARRIVAL AT SATURN

In 2004, Cassini-Huygens reached its final destination: the ringed gas giant Saturn. Since leaving Earth nearly seven years earlier, the probe had traveled almost 2.2 billion miles (3.5 billion km).

Now safely orbiting Saturn, it began beaming images and data back home with its powerful cameras and scientific instruments.

XTREME FACT – Cassini wasn't the very first spacecraft to visit Saturn. Pioneer 11 flew past the ringed planet in 1979. The Voyager 1 probe visited in 1980, followed by Voyager 2 in 1981. The images and data obtained by Cassini-Huygens, however, were far superior.

15

Cassini's cameras delighted astronomers with the most detailed images of Saturn ever seen. The spacecraft observed swirling wind patterns on the gas giant. Cassini witnessed enormous hurricanes at both the north and south poles. (Winds on Saturn can whirl at 1,118 miles per hour (1,800 kph).)

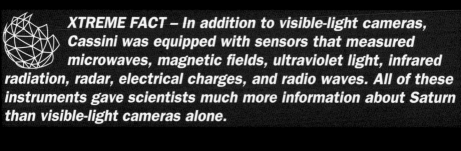

A hurricane-like storm swirls at Saturn's south pole.

XTREME FACT – In addition to visible-light cameras, Cassini was equipped with sensors that measured microwaves, magnetic fields, ultraviolet light, infrared radiation, radar, electrical charges, and radio waves. All of these instruments gave scientists much more information about Saturn than visible-light cameras alone.

The probe gave scientists the first complete view of the bizarre hexagonal cloud pattern circling Saturn's north pole. Each of the cloud's six sides is about 8,600 miles (13,840 km) long. That is longer than Earth's diameter of 7,926 miles (12,756 km).

Above: Saturn's north pole hurricane. Left: A close-up of Saturn's spinning storm. This "eye" has been measured at 1,250 miles (2,012 km) across, with cloud speeds as fast as 330 miles per hour (531 kph).

THE RINGS OF SATURN

There are seven major rings that orbit Saturn. Scientists label the innermost ring the D ring. Moving outward from the D ring are the C, B, A, F, G, and E rings. (The rings are named in the order in which they were discovered.) The rings are made almost entirely of water ice, although there are also traces of rocks. The ring particles range in size from mere dust specks to chunks of ice the size of small mountains.

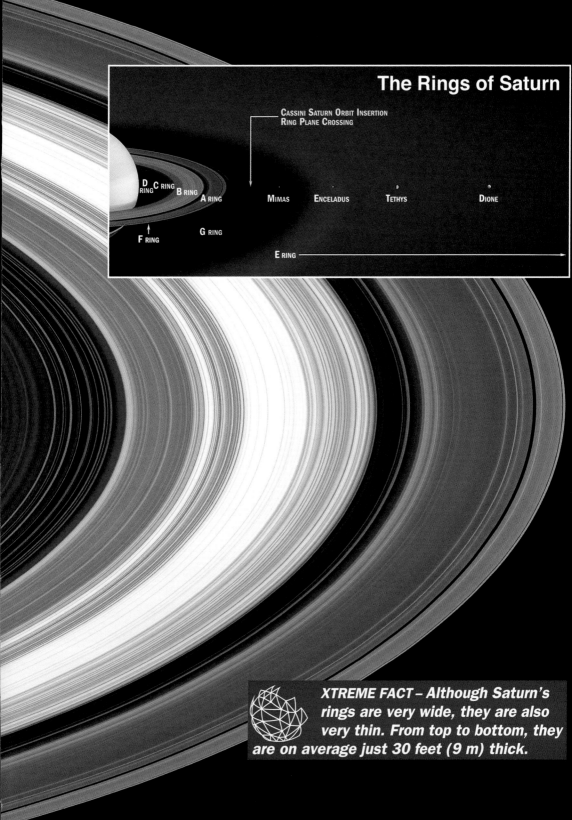

The Rings of Saturn

CASSINI SATURN ORBIT INSERTION
RING PLANE CROSSING

D RING   C RING   B RING   A RING

MIMAS   ENCELADUS   TETHYS   DIONE

F RING   G RING

E RING

XTREME FACT – Although Saturn's rings are very wide, they are also very thin. From top to bottom, they are on average just 30 feet (9 m) thick.

Cassini observed Saturn's rings for more than a decade. Scientists discovered that the ring system is dynamic and ever changing. The rings are affected by the gravity of Saturn itself and the planet's 62 known moons.

XTREME FACT – *How did Saturn's rings form? There are several theories. The rings may be material left over after Saturn was first formed. Or perhaps a moon, or several moons, were ripped apart by Saturn's gravity long ago, and the icy debris circling the planet today is all that remains.*

Collisions with comet fragments have caused ripples in some rings. The gravity of small moons has caused "propeller"-shaped gaps thousands of miles long. In 2013, scientists witnessed an icy object on the outer edge of the A ring. It may be the birth of a new Saturn moon.

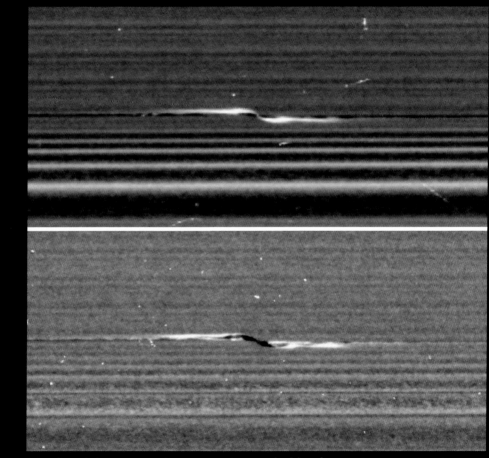

The Cassini spacecraft captured remarkable views of a propeller feature in Saturn's A ring on February 21, 2017.

TITAN

Titan is the largest of Saturn's 62 known moons. It is about the size of the planet Mercury. Titan is cloaked in a thick, nitrogen-methane haze. Cassini used special cameras and radar that peered through the smog to map Titan's surface. It revealed a world with seas of liquid methane.

Titan Dunes

There are also arid regions with windswept dunes made of water ice crystals and hydrocarbons. Most amazing of all, there is an ocean of water deep underground. Scientists say it is possible that life could be hiding under Titan's surface.

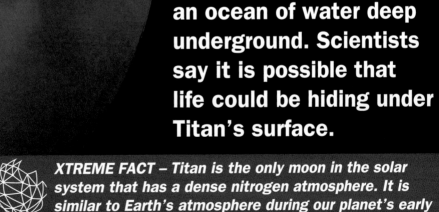

XTREME FACT – Titan is the only moon in the solar system that has a dense nitrogen atmosphere. It is similar to Earth's atmosphere during our planet's early history, before oxygen became more abundant and life arose.

THE HUYGENS PROBE

To further explore the moon Titan, Cassini carried a special hitchhiker: the Huygens probe. It was built by the European Space Agency (ESA). As Cassini flew close to Titan, Huygens separated. It landed by parachute on January 14, 2005.

XTREME FACT – *Huygens was 9 feet (2.7 m) wide, and weighed about 700 pounds (318 kg). Its outer shell protected it from burning up in Titan's atmosphere during landing. After touching down on Titan, it sent data for another 72 minutes until it lost contact with Cassini.*

As the Huygens probe descended, it beamed images back to Cassini, which relayed them to Earth. It revealed hills, ravines, and channels shaped by liquids. Huygens landed with a thud on a frozen plain where temperatures plunge to hundreds of degrees below zero. It was the first landing on a moon in the outer solar system.

MOON MYSTERIES

Besides massive Titan, Saturn has 61 other known moons. During its long mission, Cassini was able to explore most of them. There were many surprises. Enceladus has geysers in the south pole that spew water vapor. There is an ocean of water beneath its surface.

Enceladus

XTREME FACT – *Could there be life on the icy moon of Enceladus? Its underground ocean of liquid water may have the right ingredients. Future missions may tell us if life sprang up on Enceladus, and what that might teach us about the origins of life on Earth.*

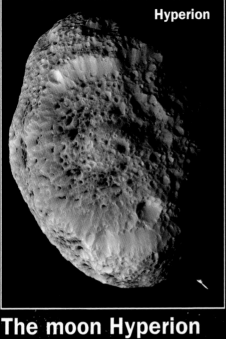

The moon Hyperion has hundreds of craters that give it a sponge-like look.

Pan is tiny and shaped like a walnut with a strange ridge around its equator.

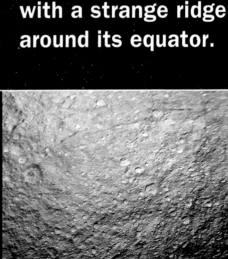

Tethys has mysterious red streaks across its surface.

THE GRAND FINALE

The **Cassini** spacecraft was wildly successful. In 2017, however, its plutonium-238 nuclear fuel was running out. Scientists gave it one final mission. It was programmed to orbit close to Saturn's rings to study them in great detail.

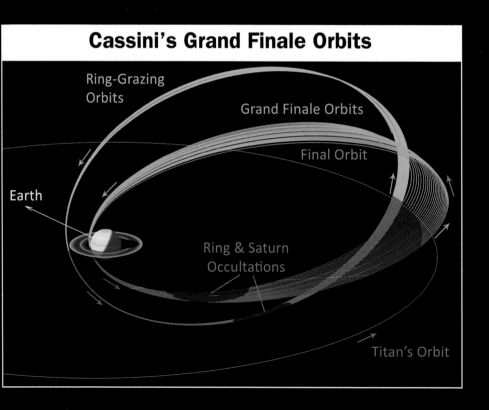

Cassini's Grand Finale Orbits

Ring-Grazing Orbits

Grand Finale Orbits

Final Orbit

Earth

Ring & Saturn Occultations

Titan's Orbit

The probe would even swoop inside the gap between Saturn and its closest ring. Finally, Cassini was programmed to plunge into Saturn's atmosphere, sending data home until its destruction.

GLOSSARY

ASTEROID BELT

A large, ring-shaped disk in the solar system, with the sun in the center. It lies between the orbits of Mars and Jupiter. It is filled with billions of rocky objects called asteroids, which range in size from mere specks to small mountains. There are many obstacles, but the amount of empty space is so vast that spacecraft have always passed safely through the asteroid belt.

EUROPEAN SPACE AGENCY (ESA)

A space agency, like NASA, that builds and flies spacecraft that explore the solar system. Its headquarters is in Paris, France. As of 2017, there are 22 countries that are members of the ESA.

FLYBY

When a spacecraft travels close to a planet or other object but does not enter into an orbit around it. During a flyby, a spacecraft has one chance to take as many photos and gather as much scientific data as possible before it sails on to its next destination.

GALILEO

Galileo Galilei was an Italian astronomer, physicist, and mathematician. He used some of the earliest telescopes to observe Saturn, Jupiter, and Venus.

HYDROCARBON
A compound that is made of hydrogen and carbon atoms. On Earth, most hydrocarbons are found in crude oil and natural gas. On Saturn's moon Titan, there are huge lakes of liquid hydrocarbons, such as methane and ethane.

MICROBE
A microscopic form of life, such as bacteria or fungi.

NATIONAL AERONAUTICS AND SPACE ADMINISTRATION (NASA)
A United States government space agency started in 1958. NASA's goals include space exploration, as well as increasing people's understanding of Earth, our solar system, and the universe.

ORBIT
The circular path a moon or spacecraft makes when traveling around a planet or other large celestial body.

PLUTONIUM-238
A highly radioactive element that produces heat. The heat is converted to electricity in a radioisotope power system, such as the one used on the Cassini spacecraft. This system is more reliable than solar panels. Radioisotope power systems produce steady, uninterrupted amounts of electricity, often for decades.

INDEX